A First Bilingual Dictionary

English/Gujarati

SCHOFIELD & SIMS LIMITED, HUDDERSFIELD, ENGLAND

Pronunciation Guide

Most Asian languages are phonetic: every phoneme (unit of sound) is represented by a particular letter. One important feature of these languages is the articulation of the consonants **d** and **t**. These are always RETROFLEX consonants in the English language, but in the Asian languages they may be DENTAL consonants.

For example
The word **d̲arjan** ('dozen' in English) is pronounced with a softer dental **d**.
The word **bot̲al** ('bottle' in English) is pronounced with a softer dental **t** .

RETROFLEX: the tongue rolls backwards and its tip touches the hard palate behind the teeth ridge.

retroflex

DENTAL: the tip of the tongue touches the inside of the upper teeth to produce a softer sound.

dental

Very many Asian words have dental consonants in them and if not correctly articulated, the pronunciation of the words is not only distorted, even the accuracy of the language may be lost.

In this book, since there are no equivalent dental consonants in the English language, where the **d**'s and **t**'s are to be pronounced DENTALLY they are <u>underlined</u> in the pronunciation guide.

A First Bilingual Dictionary

is available in five languages:

English/Bengali	0 7217 9500 5
English/Gujarati	0 7217 9501 3
English/Hindi	0 7217 9502 1
English/Punjabi	0 7217 9503 X
English/Urdu	0 7217 9504 8

© Schofield & Sims Ltd. 1995

0 7217 9501 3

First printed 1995

Design and typesetting by Armitage Typo/Graphics Ltd., Huddersfield
Translation and typesetting by Transindia, Slough

Printed and Bound in Italy by STIGE, Turin

Contents

The Body and Clothes

શરીર અને વસ્ત્રો

shareer anay vastro

arm
હાથ
haath

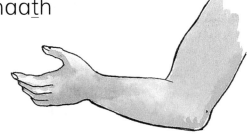

back
વાંસો
vaanso

ankle
ઘૂંટી
ghuntee

badge
બિલ્લો
billo

apron
એપરન
aypran

belt
કમરબંધ
kamarbandh

4

blouse

બ્લાઉઝ

blaaooz

boots

બુટસ

boots

buckle

બકલ

bakal

buttons

બટન

batan

cap

ટોપી

topee

cardigan

કાર્ડીગન

kaardigan

cheek

ગાલ

gaal

chest

છાતી

chhatee

chin
હડપચી
hadapachee

coat
કોટ
kot

dress
ડ્રેસ
dress

ear
કાન
kaan

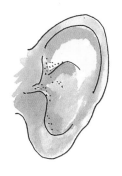

earring
એરીંગ
aering

elbow
કોણી
konee

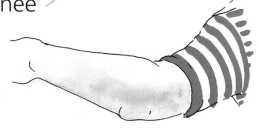

eye
આંખ
aankh

eyebrow
ભમર
bhamar

face
ચહેરો
chayhro

finger
આંગળી
aanglee

foot
પગ
pag

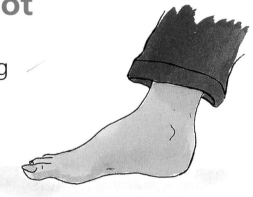

glasses
ચશ્મા
chashma

gloves
હાથ મોજાં
haath moja

hair
વાળ
vaal

hand
હાથ
haath

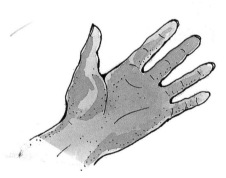

handkerchief
રૂમાલ
roomal

hat
હેટ
hat

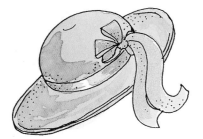

head
માથું
maathoo

helmet
હેલમેટ
haelmet

jacket
જેકેટ
jaekat

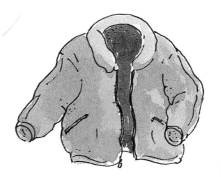

jeans
જીન્સ
jeenz

jumper
જંપર
jampar

knee
ઢીંચણ
dhichaan

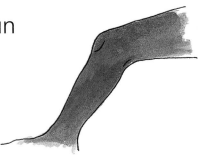

laces
દોરી
doree

leg
પગ
pag

lips
હોઠ
hotth

mouth
મોઢું
modhoo

nail
નખ
nakh

neck
ગરદન
gar<u>d</u>an

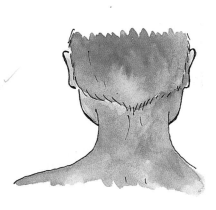

necklace
હાર
haar

nightdress
નાઇટ્રેસ
naaeetdress

nose
નાક
naak

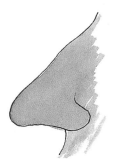

pocket
ખિસ્સું
khissoo

purse
નાણાંની કોથળી
nana bag

pyjamas
પાયજમાઝ
paajamaaz

ring
વીંટી
vinti

sari
સારી
saaree

scarf
સ્કાર્ફ
skaarf

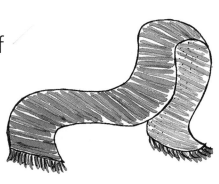

shalwar
શલવાર
shalwaar

shirt
ખમીસ
khameez

shoes
જોડા
jorda

shorts
હુંકી ચડ્ડી
tunki chaddee

shoulder
ખભો
khabho

skirt
સ્કર્ટ
skart

sock
મોજા
moja

sweatshirt
સ્વેટ શર્ટ
sweat shart

swimsuit
સ્વીમ સ્યુટ
swim soot

teeth
દાંત
daant

thumb
અંગુઠો
angootho

trainers
ટ્રેઇનર્સ
traynarz

tie
ટાઇ
taaee

trousers
પાટલુન
paṯloon

tights
ટાઇટસ
taaeets

T-shirt
ટી શર્ટ
tee shart

tongue
જિભ
jibh

tummy
પેટ
payt

turban
પાઘડી
paaghardee

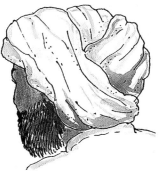

watch
નાનું ઘડીયાળ
naanu ghardiaal

umbrella
છત્રી
chha_tree

wellingtons
વેલીંગટન્સ
waelingtanz

uniform
યુનીફોર્મ
uneefaarm

wrist
કાંડુ
kaandu

vest
બંડી
bandi

zip
ઝીપ
zip

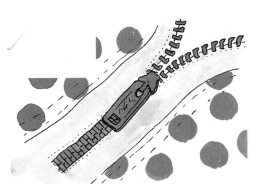

Home and Family

धर અને કુટુંબ

ghar anay kutumb

bath
બાથ
baath

battery
બેટરી
baetaree

baby
બાળક
baalak

bed
બેડ
baed

bandage
પાટો
paato

bell
ઘંટ
ghant

book
પુસ્તક
pustak

bottle
બોટલ
botal

bowl
વાટકો
vaatko

boy
છોકરો
chhokro

brother
ભાઇ
bhaaee

brush
બ્રશ
brush

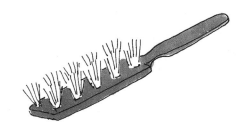

bucket
ડોલ
dol

calendar
કેલેન્ડર
kaelaendar

carpet
કારપેટ
kaarpet

clock
કલોક
klok

chair
ખુરશી
khurshee

cooker
કુકર
kukar

children
બાળકો
balako

cup
પ્યાલો
pyaalo

chimney
ચીમની
chimnee

cupboard
કબાટ
kabat

curtains

પડદા
par<u>d</u>a

cushion

તકીયો
<u>t</u>akio

daughter

દીકરી
deekree

dishwasher

ડીશવોશર
dishwaashar

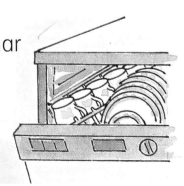

door

દરવાજો
<u>d</u>arwaajo

drawer

ખાનું
khaanoo

dustbin

ડસ્ટબીન
dastbin

father

પિતા
pi<u>t</u>a

fence

વાડ
vaard

fire

અગ્નિ
agnee

floor

ભોંયતળિયું
bhonytaliu

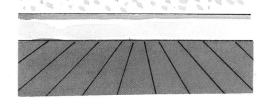

garage

ગેરેજ
gaeraj

garden

બાગ
baag

gate

ગેટ
gayt

girl

છોકરી
chhokree

glass

કાચ
kaach

glue
ગ્લુ
gloo

hose
હોઝ
hoz

grandfather
દાદા
daada

house
ધર
ghar

grandmother
દાદી
daadi

iron
ઇસ્ત્રી
istree

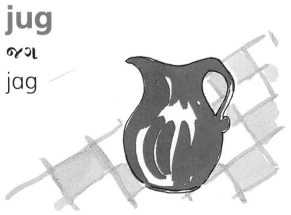

hook
વાળેલી ખીલી
valelee khilee

jug
જગ
jag

19

kettle
કીટલી
kit_lee

key
ચાવી
chaavee

knife
છરી
chharee

ladder
સીડી
seerdee

lamp
લેમ્પ
laemp

lawn
લોન
laan

light bulb
લાઇટ બલ્બ
laaeet balb

magazine
મેગેઝીન
maegazeen

man
માણસ
maanas

mirror
અરીસો
ariso

match
દીવાસળી
<u>d</u>ivasalaaee

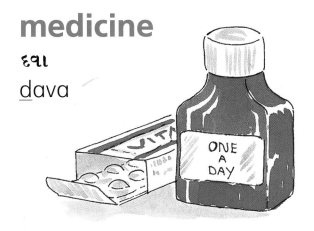

money
નાણું
naanoo

medicine
દવા
<u>d</u>ava

mother
માતા
maa<u>t</u>a

microwave
માઇક્રોવેવ
maaeekrowayv

mug
મગ
mag

needle
સોય
soay

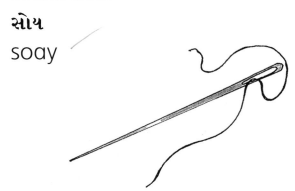

newspaper
વર્તમાન પત્ર
var_tmaan
pa_tar

paint
પેઇન્ટ
paynt

pan
કઢાઈ
kardhaaee

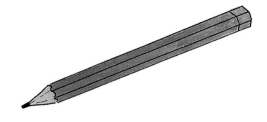

party
પાર્ટી
paartee

path
રસ્તો
ras_to

pencil
પેન્સીલ
paensil

photograph
ફોટોગ્રાફ
fotograaf

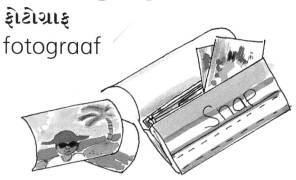

picture
ચિત્ર
chitar

plug
પ્લગ
plag

pillow
તકીયો
takio

quilt
રજાઇ
rajaaee

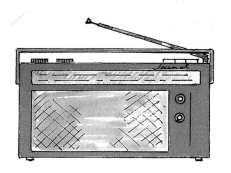

pin
પીન
pin

radio
રેડીયો
raydio

plate
પ્લેટ
playt

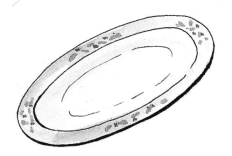

razor
રેઝર
rayzar

refrigerator

રેફ્રીજરેટર

raefreejaraytar

roof

છાપરું

chhaaproo

rubbish

કચરો

kachro

rug

ગરમ કામળો

garam
kamblo

ruler

રૂલર

roolar

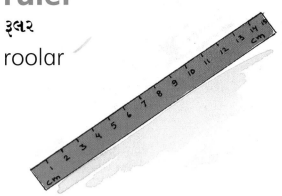

saucer

રકાબી

rakaabee

scales

સ્કેલ્સ

skaylz

scissors

કાતર

kaatar

settee
સોફા સેટ
sofa set

sink
સીન્ક
sink

shed
શેડ
shaed

sister
બહેન
baehan

shelf
શેલ્ફ
shaelf

soap
સાબુ
saaboo

shower
શાવર
shaawar

son
દીકરો
dikro

sponge
સ્પોન્જ
sponj

suitcase
સ્યુટ કેઇસ
soot kays

spoon
ચમચો
chamcho

table
મેજ
mayj

stairs
દાદરા
daadra

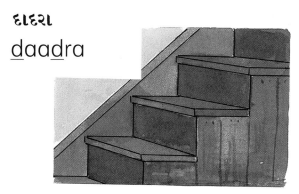

tap
ટેપ
tayp

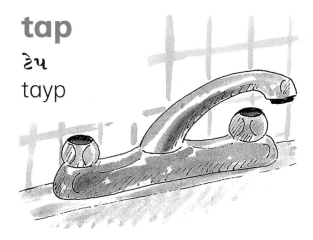

stool
સ્ટુલ
stool

telephone
ટેલીફોન
taeleefoon

television

ટેલીવીઝન

taeleeveezan

tent

તંબુ

tamboo

tin

ટીનનો ડબ્બો

tinno dabbo

toaster

ટોસ્ટર

tostar

toilet

ટોઇલેટ

toaailat

toothbrush

ટુથ બ્રશ

tuthbrash

toothpaste

ટુથ પેસ્ટ

tuth payst

torch

ટોર્ચ

torch

towel
અંગુછો
angoochho

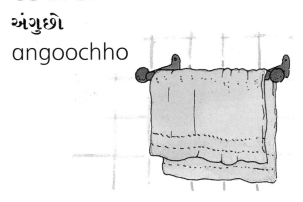

wedding
લગ્ન
lagna

vacuum cleaner
વેક્યુમ ક્લીનર
waekioom kleenar

window
બારી
baaree

video recorder
વીડીયો રેકોર્ડર
widio rikaardar

woman
સ્ત્રી
istree

washing-machine
વોશીંગ મશીન
waashing masheen

wool
ઉન
unn

Food and Drink

ખોરાક અને પીણાં

khoraak anay peena

apple
સફરજન
safarjan

banana
કેળાં
kayla

biscuit
બીસ્કીટ
biskut

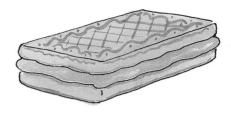

bread
રોટલી
rotlee

butter
માખણ
makhan

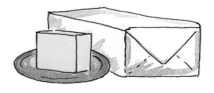

cabbage
કોબીજ
kobij

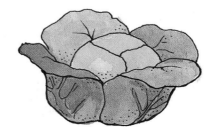

cake
કેઇક
kayk

carrot
ગાજર
gaajar

cauliflower
કોલી ફલાવર
kolee falaawar

cereal
કઠોળ
kathord

chapatti
ચપાટી
chapaatee

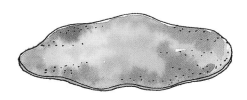

cheese
પનીર
paneer

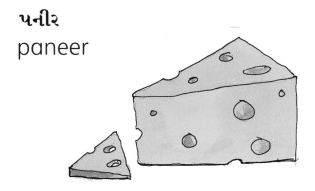

cherry
ચેરી
chaeree

chocolate
ચોકલેટ
chaaklayt

30

coffee
કોફી
kofee

egg
ઈંડા
anda

cream
ક્રીમ
kreem

fish
માછલી
maachhlee

crisps
ક્રીસ્પસ
krisps

flour
લોટ
lot

cucumber
કાકડી
kaakrdee

grapefruit
ગ્રેઈપ ફ્રુટ
grayp froot

grapes

દ્રાક્ષ

draaksh

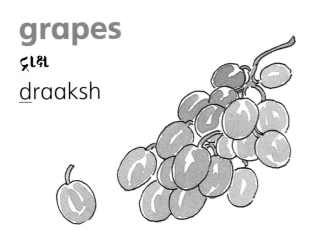

hamburger

હામ બર્ગર

haam bargar

honey

મધ

madh

ice-cream

આઇસક્રીમ

aaeeskreem

jam

જમ

jam

jelly

જેલી

jaelee

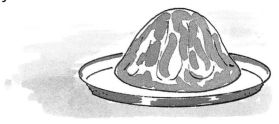

lemon

લીંબુ

limboo

lettuce

લેટસ

laetas

loaf
રોટલો
rotlo

milk
દૂધ
du̲dh̲

margarine
માર્જરીન
maarjareen

mushroom
બીલાડીનો ટોપ
bilaadino top

meat
મીટ
meet

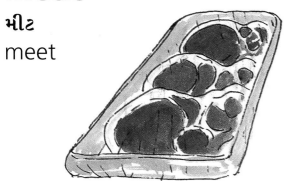

onion
ડુંગળી
dungaree

melon
તરબુચ
t̲arbuch

orange
નારંગી
naarangee

pancake
પાનકેઇક
paankayk

pasta
પાસ્ટા
paasta

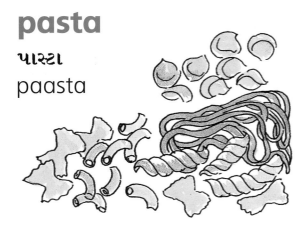

peach
પીચ
peech

pear
જમરૂખ
jarmukh

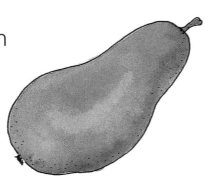

peas
વટાણા
vatana

pepper
મરી
maree

pickle
અથાણું
a_thaanoo

picnic
પીકનીક
piknik

34

pie
પાઇ
paaee

pop
પોપ
pop

pineapple
અનાનસ
anaanas

potato
બટેટા
batayta

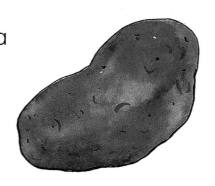

pizza
પીઝ્ઝા
piza

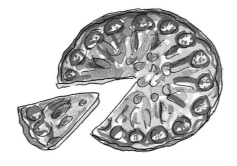

pudding
પુડીંગ
puding

plum
જરદાલુ
jardaaloo

rice
ચોખા
chokha

salad
સાલાડ
salaad

soup
સૂપ
soop

salt
મીઠું
mithoo

spaghetti
સ્પગેટી
spaegaetee

sandwich
સેન્ડવીચ
saendwich

strawberry
સ્ટ્રોબેરી
straabaree

sauce
સોસ
sos

sugar
ખાંડ
khaand

sweets
મિઠાઈ
mithaaee

tangerine
નારંગી
naarangi

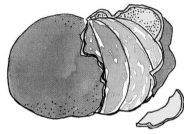

tea
ચા
cha

toast
ટોસ્ટ
tost

tomato
ટોમેટો
tamaato

vegetable
શાકભાજી
shaakbhaajee

water
પાણી
paanee

yoghurt
દહીં
<u>d</u>ahee

Living Creatures

જીવતાં પ્રાણીઓ

jivto praanio

badger
બેજર
baejar

bear
રીંછ
rinchha

beetle
વાંદો
vaan<u>d</u>o

bird
પક્ષી
pakshee

butterfly
પતંગિયું
pa<u>t</u>angiu

camel
ઉંટ
oonta

38

cat
બિલાડી
bilaardee

caterpillar
કેટરપીલર
kaytarpillar

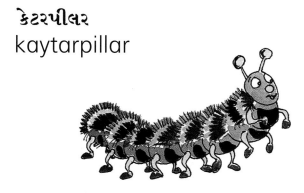

cow
ગાય
gaaay

crab
કરચલો
karachlo

crocodile
મગર
magar

deer
હરણ
haran

dog
કુતરો
kutro

dolphin
ડોલ્ફીન
dolfin

donkey
ગધેડો
gadhayrdo

duck
બતક
batak

eagle
ગરુડ
garurd

elephant
હાથી
haathee

fish
માછલી
maachhlee

fly
માખી
maakhee

fox
શિયાળ
shiyaal

frog
દેડકો
daydko

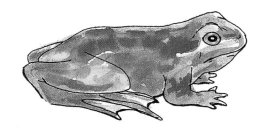

giraffe

જિરાફ

jiraaf

gorilla

મોટો વાંદરો

moto
vaan<u>d</u>ro

goat

બકરો

bakro

guinea-pig

મોટા ઉંદર જેવું પ્રાણી

mota un<u>d</u>ar jiv
praanee

goldfish

સોનેરી માછલી

sonayree
maachhlee

hedgehog

શેળો

shaylo

goose

હંસ

hans

hen

મરઘી

marghee

41

hippopotamus

જળઘોડો
jalghordo

horse

ઘોડો
ghordo

insect

જીવડું
jivdoo

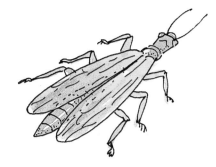

kangaroo

કાંગારુ
kangaroo

ladybird

ગોળ જીવડું
gol jivdoo

leopard

ચિત્તો
chitto

lion

સિંહ
sin

lizard

ધરોળી
gharolee

lobster
કરચલો
karachlo

ostrich
શાહમૃગ
shaahmurg

monkey
વાંદરો
vaan<u>d</u>ro

owl
ઘુવડ
ghuvard

mouse
ઉંદર
un<u>d</u>er

panda
પાન્ડા
paanda

octopus
દરિયાનું પાણી
<u>d</u>ariyaanoo praanee

parrot
પોપટ
popat

penguin
પેનગ્વિન
paengooin

sheep
ઘેટું
ghaytoo

rabbit
સસલું
sasloo

snail
ગોકળગાય
gokalgaaay

rhinoceros
ગેંડો
gayndo

snake
સાપ
saap

shark
શાર્ક માછલી
shaark
maachhlee

spider
કરોળીયો
karolio

squirrel
ખીસકોલી
khiskoli

wasp
ભમરો
bhamro

swan
રાજહંસ
raajhans

whale
વ્હેલ માછલી
wayl maachhlee

tiger
વાઘ
vaagh

wolf
વરૂ
varoo

tortoise
કાચબો
kachaabo

zebra
ઝીબ્રા
zaybra

Plants

છોડવાઓ

chhordvao

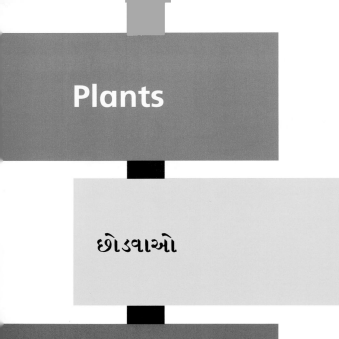

daffodil
પીળું પુષ્પ
peeloo
pushp

daisy
ડેઇઝી નામનું પુષ્પ
dayzee
pushp

bush
ઝાડી
zaardee

flower
પુષ્પ
pushp

cactus
થોર
<u>t</u>hor

forest
જંગલ
jangal

grass
ધાસ
ghaas

seaweed
દરીયાનો છોડ
dariyanoo chhord

leaf
પાંદડું
paanddu

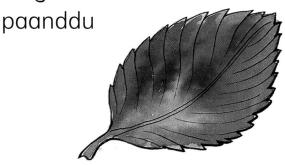

seed
બીયાં
biyan

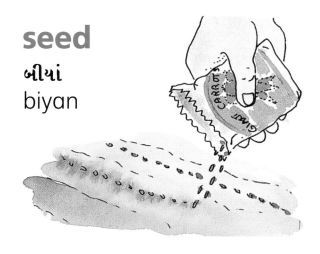

root
મૂળિયું
muliyoo

sunflower
સુરજમુખી
sooraj mukhee

rose
ગુલાબ
gulaab

tree
ઝાડ
zaard

Weather and Seasons

હવામાન અને ઋતુઓ

havaamaan anay rutuo

autumn

પાનખર

pankhar

cloud

વાદળું

vaadloo

flood

રેલ

rayl

fog

ધુમ્મસ

dhummas

rain

વરસાદ

varsaad

rainbow

મેઘધનુષ્ય

mayghdhanush

sky
આકાશ
aakaash

snow
બરફ
baraf

spring
વસંત
vasan<u>t</u>

storm
તોફાન
<u>t</u>oofaan

summer
ઉનાળો
unaalo

sun
સૂરજ
sooraj

wind
પવન
pavan

winter
શિયાળો
shiaalo

Natural Features

કુદરતી સર્જનો

kudartee
sarjano

desert
રણ
ran

earthquake
ધરતીકંપ
dharteekum

cave
ગુફા
gufa

island
ટાપુ
taapoo

cliff
ઊભી ટેકરી
ubhi taykree

lake
સરોવર
sarovar

mountain
પર્વત
parva<u>t</u>

river
નદી
na<u>d</u>i

sand
રેતી
ray<u>t</u>ee

sea
દરીયો
<u>d</u>ariaao

soil
જમીન
jameen

volcano
જવાળામુખી
jwalamukhee

waterfall
પાણીનો ધોધ
paanino
<u>dh</u>o<u>dh</u>

waves
પાણીના મોજાં
paanina
mojan

Space

અવકાશ

avkaash

moon
ચંદ્ર
chan<u>d</u>ra

rocket
રોકેટ
raaket

comet
કોમેટ
komet

satellite
સેટેલાઇટ
saetaylaaeet

Earth
જમીન
jameen

stars
તારા
<u>t</u>aara

People at Work

ધંધાદારી માણસો

dhandhaari manaso

baker
ભઠિયારો
bhathiaaro

builder
બાંધકામ કરનારો
bandhkaam karno

acrobat
ગોડીયો
godio

businessman
વેપારી
vaypaaree

artist
કળાકાર
kalaakaar

butcher
કસાઇ
kasaaee

carpenter
સુથાર
suthaar

doctor
ડોકટર
daaktar

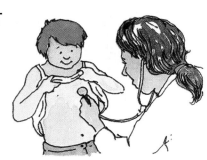

cook
રસોયો
rasoeeo

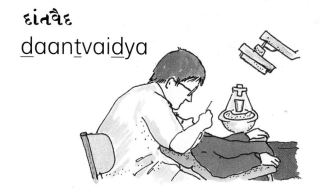

electrician
ઇલેકટ્રીસીઅન
eelaektreeshan

dentist
દાંતવૈદ
daantvaidya

farmer
ખેડુત
khaydut

diver
મરજીવો
marajeevo

fire-fighter
આગ હોલવનાર
aag holavnaar

fisherman

માછીમાર

maachheemaar

lorry driver

લોરી ડ્રાઇવર

laaree
draaeevar

gardener

માળી

maalee

mechanic

મિકેનીક

makaenik

hairdresser

હેર ડ્રેસર

hayardresar

musician

ગવૈયો

gavaeeo

judge

જજ

jaj

nurse

નર્સ

nars

people

પ્રજા

praja

pilot

પાઇલટ

paailat

plumber

નળ સમારનાર

nal
samarnaar

policeman

પોલીસમેન

poleesman

policewoman

પોલીસવુમન

poleeswoman

postman

ટપાલી

tapalee

sailor

ખલાસી

khalaasee

scientist

વિજ્ઞાનશાસ્ત્રી

vigyanshaastree

secretary
સેક્રેટરી
saekraytaree

train driver
ટ્રેઇન ડ્રાઇવર
trayn
draaeevar

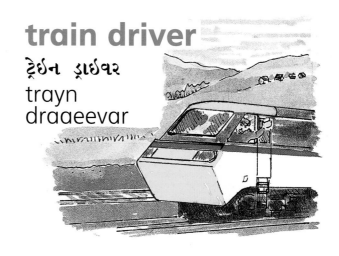

shopkeeper
દુકાનદાર
dukaandaar

vet
જનાવરનો ડોકટર
jaanvarno
daaktar

soldier
લશ્કરી સિપાઇ
laskarno
sipahee

waiter
વેઇટર
waytar

teacher
શિક્ષક
shikshak

waitress
વેઇટરસ
waytraes

Places we Visit

મુલાકાત લેવાના સ્થળો

mulaakaat
levana sthalo

cinema
સીનેમા
sinayma

factory
કારખાનું
kaarkhaanoo

bank
બેંક
baenk

farm
ફાર્મ
faarm

church
દેવળ
deval

fire station
ફાયરસ્ટેશન
faairstayshan

58

hospital
હોસ્પીટલ
hospeetal

hotel
હોટેલ
hotal

library
લાયબ્રેરી
laaibrayree

market
માર્કેટ
maarkit

mosque
મસ્જિદ
masjid

museum
મ્યુઝીયમ
meeoozeeam

office
ઓફ્ીસ
aafis

park
પાર્ક
paark

59

police station

પોલીસ સ્ટેશન

polees stayshan

school

સ્કુલ

skool

post office

પોસ્ટ ઓફીસ

post aafis

shop

દુકાન

<u>d</u>ukaan

queue

લાઇન

laaeen

sports centre

સ્પોર્ટ સેન્ટર

sport saentar

restaurant

રેસ્ટોરન્ટ

raestorant

supermarket

સુપરમાર્કેટ

supar maarket

Transport and Communications

વાહનો અને પત્રવ્યવહાર

vaahno anay
patravyavhaar

aeroplane
એરોપ્લેન
aeroplayn

airport
એરપોર્ટ
aerport

ambulance
એમ્બ્યુલન્સ
aemboolans

balloon
ફુગ્ગો
fuggo

barge
પડાઉ
pardaao

bicycle
બાઇસીકલ
baaeesikal

61

boat
મછવો
machhavo

car
કાર
kaar

bridge
પૂલ
pul

caravan
કારાવાન
kaaravaan

bus
બસ
bas

car park
કાર પાર્ક
kaar paark

canoe
નાની હોડી
naani hordi

coach
કોચ
koch

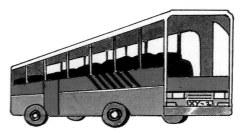

engine
એન્જિન
injin

envelope
પરબીડીયું
parbidiu

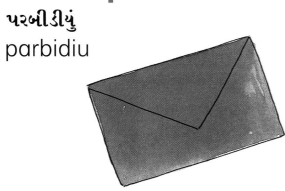

fax machine
ફેક્ષ મશીન
faeks
masheen

ferry
ફેરી
fayree

fire-engine
ફાયર એન્જિન
faair injin

helicopter
હેલીકોપ્ટર
haeleekaaptar

letter
પત્ર
patar

lift
લીફ્ટ
lift

lighthouse
લાઇટ હાઉસ
laaeet haaoos

oar
હલેસું
halaysoo

lorry
લોરી
laaree

parachute
પેરેશુટ
paeraashoot

motorbike
મોટરબાઇક
motarbaaeek

parcel
પાર્સલ
paarsal

motorway
મોટર વે
motar way

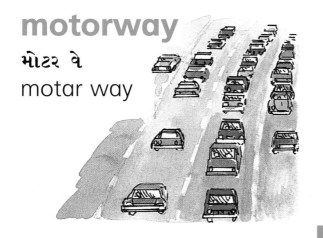

passenger
મુસાફર
musaafar

petrol pump
પેટ્રોલ પંપ
paetrol pamp

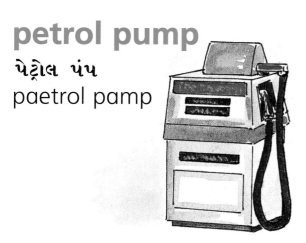

road
રસ્તો
rasto

platform
પ્લેટફોર્મ
plaetfaarm

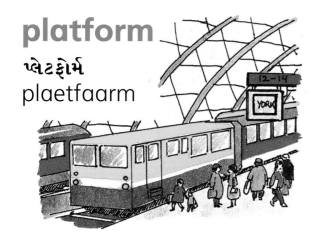

ship
વહાણ
vaahan

police car
પોલીસ કાર
polees kaar

stamp
સ્ટેમ્પ
staemp

racing car
રેસીંગ કાર
raysing kaar

station
સ્ટેશન
stayshan

submarine
સબમરીન
sabmareen

telephone box
ટેલીફોન બોક્ષ
taeleefon boksh

tanker
ટેંકર
taenkar

ticket
ટીકીટ
tikat

taxi
ટેક્ષી
taeksee

tractor
ટ્રેકટર
traektar

telephone
ટેલીફોન
taeleefon

traffic lights
ટ્રાફીક લાઇટ
traefik laaeet

trailer
ટ્રેઇલર
traylar

train
ટ્રેઇન
trayn

tunnel
ભોંયરૂ
bhoyaroo

van
વાન
waan

wagon
વેગન
waegan

wheel
પૈડું
paydoo

wheelchair
વ્હીલચેર
weelchayar

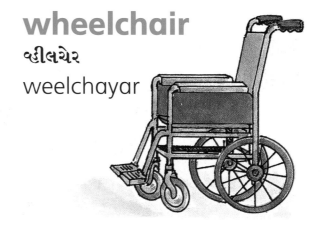

yacht
યોટ
yaat

Tools and Machines

ઓજારો અને મશીનો

ojaaro anay masheeno

computer
કોમ્પ્યુટર
kampeeootar

crane
ક્રેઇન
krayn

calculator
કેલ્ક્યુલેટર
kaelkoolaytar

camera
કેમેરા
kaemra

digger
ડીગર
digar

drill
ડ્રીલ
dril

hammer
હથોડો
hathordo

sewing machine
સીવવાનું મશીન
sivvanoo masheen

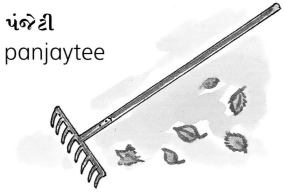

rake
પંજેટી
panjaytee

spade
કોદાળી
kodari

saw
કરવત
karvat

spanner
સ્પેનર
spaenar

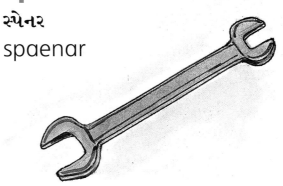

screwdriver
સ્ક્રૂ ડ્રાઇવર
skroo draaeevar

typewriter
ટાઇપરાઇટર
taaeep raaeetar

Toys, Games and Musical Instruments

રમકડાં, રમતો અને ગાયનો વગાડવાના સાધનો

ramakada, rama_to anay gayano vagadvana saa_dhno

bat
બેટ
baet

bicycle
બાઇસીકલ
baaeesikal

ball
દડો
_dado

bricks
બ્રીક્સ
briks

balloon
ફુગ્ગો
fuggo

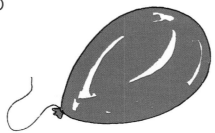

cards
કાર્ડ્સ
kaardz

chess
શેતરંજ
shatranj

dancing
નૃત્ય
nritya

comic
કોમીક
komik

dice
પાસા
paasa

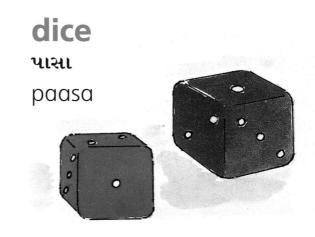

crayons
કેયન્સ
krayanz

draughts
ડ્રાફ્ટસ
draafts

cricket
ક્રિકેટ
krikat

drum
ડ્રમ
dram

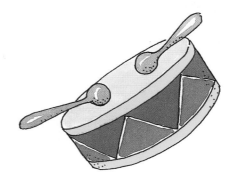

flute
વાંસળી
vaanslee

football
ફુટબોલ
futbaal

golf
ગોલ્ફ
golf

guitar
ગીટાર
gitaar

gymnastics
જિમનાસ્ટીક્સ
jimnaastiks

harp
હાર્પ
haarp

horse riding
ધોડેસવારી
ghordsav-
aaree

jigsaw
જગસો
jigsaa

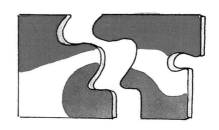

jumping
કૂદવાની રમત
kud̲vanee
ramat̲

kite
પતંગ
pat̲ang

mask
બુરખો
burkho

paintbrush
પેઇન્ટ બ્રશ
paynt brush

paints
પેઇન્ટસ
paynts

piano
પીઆનો
peeaano

puppet
ઢીંગલી
dhinglee

recorder
રેકોર્ડર
rikaardar

roller boots

રોલર બુટસ

rolar boots

seesaw

સી શો

see shaa

roundabout

રાઉન્ડ એબાઉટ

raaoond
abaaoot

skipping-rope

સ્કીપીંગ રોપ

skiping rop

rounders

રાઉન્ડર્સ

raaoondarz

slide

સ્લાઇડ

slaaeed

running

દોડવું

<u>d</u>ordvoo

swimming

તરવું

<u>t</u>arvoo

swing
ઝૂલવું
zulvoo

table tennis
ટેબલ ટેનિસ
taybal taenis

tambourine
ટેમ્બોરાઇન
tamboreen

tennis
ટેનીસ
taenis

trombone
ટ્રોમ્બોન
trombon

trumpet
રણશિંગુ
ranshingoo

violin
વાયોલીન
waailin

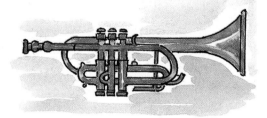

xylophone
ઝાઇલોફોન
zaaeelofon

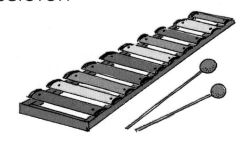

75

Fantasy and Imagination

ખ્વાબ અને કલ્પનાઓ

khwaab anay
kalpanaao

angel
દેવદૂત
dayvdoot

cannon
તોપ
top

castle
કીલ્લો
kilo

circus
સર્કસ
sarkas

clown
વિદૂષક
vidooshak

crown
તાજ
taaj

dragon
લશ્કરી સિપાઇ
lashkari sipaaee

magician
જાદુગર
jaadoogar

ghost
ભૂત
bhoot

monster
દૈત્ય
daetya

giant
રાક્ષસ
raakhshas

palace
મહેલ
mahal

king
રાજા
raaja

pirate
ચાંચિયો
chaancheeo

77

prince
રાજકુંવર
raajkunvar

princess
રાજકુંવરી
raajkunvaree

prison
કેદખાનું
kaedkhaanoo

queen
રાણી
raani

sword
તલવાર
talwaar

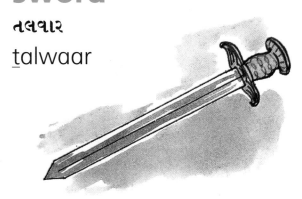

treasure
ખજાનો
khajano

witch
ડાકણ
daakan

wizard
જાદુગર
jaadoogar

Numbers and Shapes

આંકડા અને આકારો

aankrda anay
aakaaro

one
એક
ayk

two
બે
bay

three
ત્રણ
taran

four
ચાર
chaar

five
પાંચ
paanch

six
છ
chha

seven
સાત
saat

eight
આઠ
aath

nine
નવ
nav
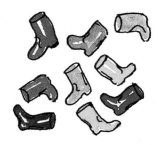

ten
દશ
dash

eleven
અગિયાર
agiaar

twelve
બાર
baar

thirteen
તેર
_tayr

fourteen
ચૌદ
chau_d

fifteen
પંદર
pan_dar

sixteen
સોળ
sol

seventeen
સત્તર
sa_t_tar

eighteen
અઢાર
adhar

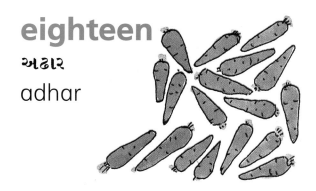

nineteen
ઓગણીસ
ognees

twenty
વીસ
vees

circle

ગોળ
gol

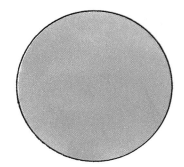

cube

ક્યુબ
keeoob

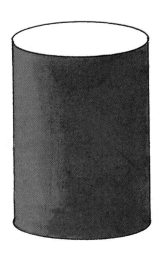

cylinder

સીલીન્ડર
silindar

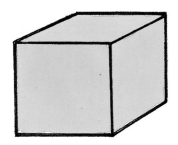

diamond

ડાયમંડ
daaimand

oval

લંબગોળ
lambgol

rectangle

રેકટેંગલ
raektaengal

square

ચોરસ
choras

triangle

ત્રીકોણ
t̲rikon

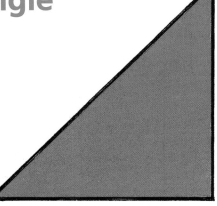

Time

સમય

samay

Monday
સોમ
som

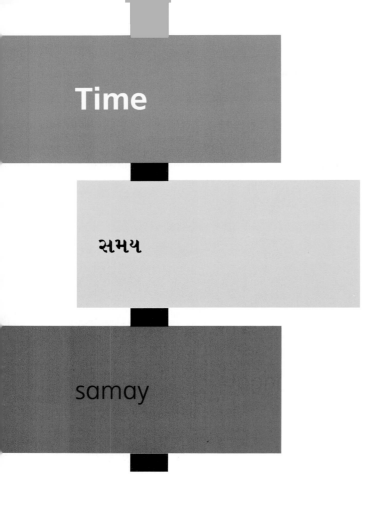

OCTOBER 3
Monday

BOB'S PAPER ROUND

UNCLE HENRY COMES FOR TEA

Tuesday
મંગળ
mangal

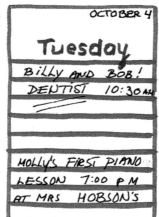

OCTOBER 4
Tuesday

BILLY AND BOB! DENTIST 10:30 AM

MOLLY'S FIRST PIANO LESSON 7:00 PM AT MRS HOBSON'S

Wednesday
બુધ
bu_dh

OCTOBER 5
Wednesday

UNCLE DAVE'S BIRTHDAY !

Thursday
ગુરૂ
guroo

OCTOBER 6
Thursday

CINEMA !

BUY: BREAD CAT FOOD CHEESE

Friday
શુક્ર
shukra

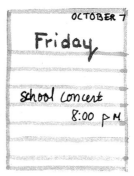

OCTOBER 7
Friday

school concert 8:00 PM

Saturday
શનિ
shanee

OCTOBER 8
Saturday

GRANDMA'S PARTY. RING AUNTIE FLORA SHE LEFT HER HAT IN DAD'S CAR.

Sunday
રવિ
ravee

OCTOBER 9
Sunday

Mum's birthday!

January
જાન્યુઆરી
januwaree

February
ફેબ્રુઆરી
faruwaree

March
માર્ચ
maarch

April
એપ્રિલ
aypril

May
મે
may

June
જુન
joon

July
જુલાઇ
joolaaee

August
ઓગસ્ટ
aagas<u>t</u>

September
સપ્ટેમ્બર
saeptambar

October
ઓક્ટોબર
oktobar

November
નવેમ્બર
navambar

December
ડિસેમ્બર
disambar

daytime
દિવસનો સમય
divasno samay

afternoon
દિવસનો પાછલો પહોર
divasno paachhlo pahor

night-time
રાત્રીનો સમય
raatrino samay

evening
સાંજ
saanj

morning
સવાર
sawaar

sunrise
સૂર્યોદય
suryoday

midday
મધ્યાહન
madhyahan

sunset
સૂર્યાસ્ત
suryoast

o'clock

સાત વાગે

saat vajay

breakfast

નાસ્તો

naashto

half-past

સાડા

saarday

lunch

બપોરનું જમવાનું

bopornoo
jamwaanoo

quarter-past

સવા

sava

tea

ચા

cha

quarter to

પોણા નવ વાગે

ponay nav
vajay

supper

છેલ્લું ખાણું

chhayloo
bhojan

Colours

રંગો

rango

gold
સોનેરી
soneree

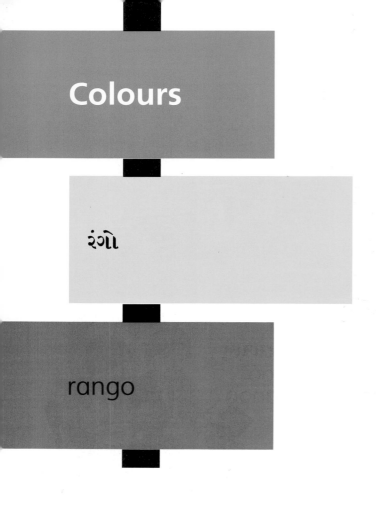

silver
ચાંદી
chaandee

black
કાળું
kaaloo

blue
વાદળી
vaa_d_lee

brown
બદામી
baa_d_aamee

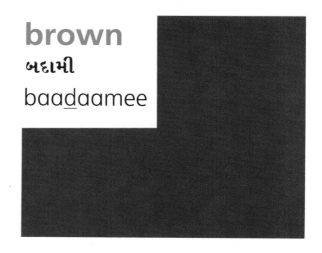

green
ચાંદી
liloo

grey
ભૂખરું
bhukhroo

red
લાલ
laal

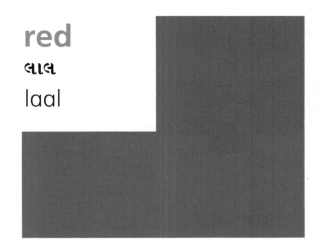

orange
નારંગી
naarangee

violet
જાંબુડી
jamburdee

pink
ગુલાબી
gulaabee

white
સફેદ
safay<u>d</u>

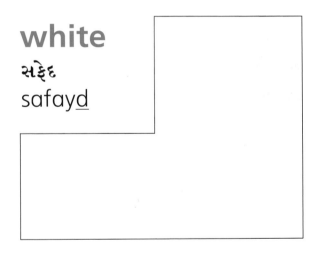

purple
જાંબુડી લાલ
jamburdi laal

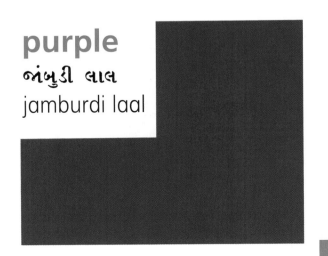

yellow
પીળું
peeloo

Adjectives

વિશેષણો

vishayshan

back
પાછળનો
pachhaalno

front
આગળનો
aagalno

clean
સાફ
saaf

dirty
ગંદુ
gandoo

cold
ઠંડું
thandoo

hot
ગરમ
garam

empty
ખાલી
khaalee

full
ભરેલું
bharaysoo

fast
ઉતાવળથી
u_tavalt_hee

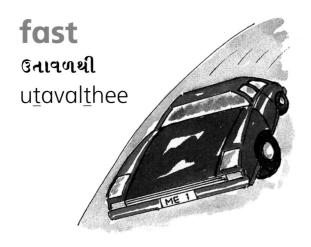

slow
ધીમું
dhimoo

happy
સુખી
sukhee

sad
દીલગીર
_dilgeer

heavy
વજનદાર
vajan_daar

light
હલકું
halkoo

large
મોટું
motoo

small
નાનું
naanoo

long
લાંબું
laamboo

short
ટૂંકું
tunkoo

narrow
સાંકડું
saankrdoo

wide
પહોળું
paholoo

old
વૃધ્ધ
vrudhaa

young
જુવાન
juwaan

90

Word list

Aa

acrobat	53
aeroplane	61
afternoon	84
airport	61
ambulance	61
angel	76
ankle	4
apple	29
April	83
apron	4
arm	4
artist	53
August	83
autumn	48

Bb

baby	14
back	4, 88
badge	4
badger	38
baker	53
ball	70
balloon	61, 70
banana	29
bandage	14
bank	58
barge	61
bat	70
bath	14
battery	14
bear	38
bed	14
beetle	38
bell	14
belt	4
bicycle	61, 70
bird	38
biscuit	29

black	86
blouse	5
blue	86
boat	62
book	15
boots	5
bottle	15
bowl	15
boy	15
bread	29
breakfast	85
bricks	70
bridge	62
brother	15
brown	86
brush	15
bucket	15
buckle	5
builder	53
bus	62
bush	46
businessman	53
butcher	53
butter	29
butterfly	38
buttons	5

Cc

cabbage	29
cactus	46
cake	30
calculator	68
calendar	15
camel	38
camera	68
cannon	76
canoe	62
cap	5
car	62
caravan	62
cardigan	5

cards	70
car park	62
carpenter	54
carpet	16
carrot	30
castle	76
cat	39
caterpillar	39
cauliflower	30
cave	50
cereal	30
chair	16
chapatti	30
cheek	5
cheese	30
cherry	30
chess	71
chest	5
children	16
chimney	16
chin	6
chocolate	30
church	58
cinema	58
circle	81
circus	76
clean	88
cliff	50
clock	16
cloud	48
clown	76
coach	62
coat	6
coffee	31
cold	88
comet	52
comic	71
computer	68
cook	54
cooker	16
cow	39
crab	39

Hh

hair	7
hairdresser	55
half-past	85
hamburger	32
hammer	69
hand	7
handkerchief	7
happy	89
harp	72
hat	8
head	8
heavy	89
hedgehog	41
helicopter	63
helmet	8
hen	41
hippopotamus	42
honey	32
hook	19
horse	42
horse riding	72
hose	19
hospital	59
hot	88
hotel	59
house	19

Ii

ice-cream	32
insect	42
iron	19
island	50

Jj

jacket	8
jam	32
January	83
jeans	8
jelly	32
jigsaw	72
judge	55
jug	19
July	83
jumper	8
jumping	73
June	83

Kk

kangaroo	42
kettle	20
key	20
king	77
kite	73
knee	8
knife	20

Ll

laces	8
ladder	20
ladybird	42
lake	50
lamp	20
large	90
lawn	20
leaf	47
leg	9
lemon	32
leopard	42
letter	63
lettuce	32
library	59
lift	63
light	89
light bulb	20
lighthouse	64
lion	42
lips	9
lizard	42
loaf	33
lobster	43
long	90
lorry	64
lorry driver	55
lunch	85

Mm

magazine	20
magician	77
man	21
March	83
margarine	33
market	59
mask	73
match	21
May	83
meat	33
mechanic	55
medicine	21
melon	33
microwave	21
midday	84
milk	33
mirror	21
Monday	82
money	21
monkey	43
monster	77
Months of the year:	83
moon	52
morning	84
mosque	59
mother	21
motorbike	64
motorway	64
mountain	51
mouse	43
mouth	9
mug	21
museum	59
mushroom	33
musician	55

Nn

nail	9
narrow	90
neck	9
necklace	9
needle	22
newspaper	22